Through The Eyes of George

By John Steuber

For more information on *Through The Eyes of George* visit the podcast and YouTube channel also called *Through The Eyes of George* and the website www.potus1.com

This book is dedicated to the woman that is to be my Martha Washington.

CONTENTS

Introduction   11
The Sculpture of Character   16
Real Fake News   32
You Set Your Own Destiny   35
Family and Friends   47
Military   54
Worry About Yourself First   60
Religious Toleration   70
Holding Back the Tide   76
Bibliography   95
Reference Notes   99

INTRODUCTION

Sometimes the truth is hard to hear. And sometimes people want to remain ignorant or remain arrogant because they don't want to listen to the fact or they don't know how to get to the truth. Maybe the authenticity of any topic is being kept from a group of people. In either case, we are reminded of a scene in "A Few Good Men" when Tom Cruise's character is talking to Jack Nickelson's role in the courtroom. Jack says to Tom's character when presented with all the facts, "you can't handle the truth." And that's true in some cases.

I know there are times in my life that I have been presented with all the facts or truths on a matter, and I could not handle it and could not accept it. But I got through it and moved forward. George Washington was an honest man, but at times he had to be like Tom Cruise's character was. George Washington wanted people to act with dignity and loyalty. He was though, very hurt when his friend and subordinate Benedict Arnold betrayed him. George didn't want to believe it. But George knew what he must do in the aftermath and truth of Arnold's betrayal.

What do you think of when you picture an ideal leader, father, patriot, friend or believer? George Washington, with high magnitude, changed the world forever because he believed first and foremost that he was more than a conqueror in the most unfathomable circumstances. George would see the big picture in a culturally tumultuous time like a thunderstorm with no end in sight. Just as today seems uncertain and cloudy, we need and can see the big picture and persevere through all and any situations, just as George did. Our believing images of victory can and will carry us to our goals.

What made George this confident? What would George think about our current political situations? Have you considered what President Washington would do when insurmountable odds were thrust upon him with a congressional deadlock that needed immediate attention? George had many times during his presidency a Congress that could not act quickly, but he persevered. What's the point in the 50 state governments and other U.S. territories if the Federal Government always steps in? That is like having parents always step in and answer for kids, even if the kids are 80 years old like the "helicopter parents" of today.

George Washington was a man of integrity, loyalty, and prudence. We see that Washington wanted nothing more than to be at Mount Vernon with his beloved Martha in a letter that he wrote to her on June 18, 1775. But duty, honor, and service called him to set the conversation and shift the paradigm in a turbulent new world. Today is no different. Every day is tumultuous if we can't renew our minds to the truth of our spiritual beliefs, the words in the Constitution, the words in the Declaration of Independence, and the words in the Federalist Papers. In this book, we will examine how "George would address" life and politics of today contrasting experiences within his own era.

Some people say that George Washington was a deist and not a Christian. Washington believed in a higher power, providence or "mighty hand" of creation whether that's deist or Christian, WHO CARES! He believed in God and prayed fervently and daily. He was tolerant of other people's religious beliefs as we see in a letter written in August 1790 to the Hebrew congregation in Newport and other places he spoke. Washington desired that all people in the colonies would have the opportunity to thrive and achieve their dreams peacefully and harmoniously.

George believed in the unity that would come from the strength of the states individually and not solely always relying on the Federal Government. He thought modestly that all people have the right to be free. George believed in bringing people together to change the world, so eventually, all people can be free and live a powerful and more than abundant life, if they choose to.

In this book, we will go on an adventure through the eyes of George Washington, and at times we will call him George because that's who he was. A human, with flaws. He was the man that the whole world looked up to. And he was not a demi-god or deity in a fictional reality.

Furthermore, we'll examine many topics and ask a myriad of questions close to our hearts through each chapter. We will explore issues that, at times, may seem far and distant in resolution within our current culture and others that still align. We will examine the facts and moments experienced by George and understand what President Washington might have done or did to procure the rendezvous with the destiny of the city on a hill that is the United States.

My goal in this short writing adventure about George Washington is to get straight to the salient facts. If I were to suggest a few other longer George Washington biographies that are many more pages in length I would recommend:

"Washington's God" by Michael and Jana Novak
"Washington on Washington" by Paul M. Zall
"First Entrepreneur" by Edward Lengel
"George Washington First in War First in Peace" by James Crutcheld
"Mr. President" by Harlow Giles Unger
George Washington's Mount Vernon the Official guidebook (edition 2017)

THE SCULPTURE OF CHARACTER

George Washington was the physical manifestation, an embodiment of everything internally that human beings desire to be for themselves, for their communities, for their families, for their neighbors, for their confidants, for their coworkers, and anybody else that we meet.

The reason why Washington was so important back in his time and culture, as well as our time in 2019 and our culture, is because he was looked up to like a demi-god. George, (as we will affectionately call him at times in this book), was a man with many medical ailments. He always tried to embody the character traits of honor, dignity, duty, sacrifice, commitment, faithfulness, chivalry and civility. People in his time, throughout all of time and in today's culture which try to embody those character traits but can't seem to have a steady grasp of a consistent relationship of a robust sculptural character of themselves.

Washington made many mistakes in his life, but nobody wants to be remembered for their mistakes even George Washington.

During Washington's first term as President of the United States, he knew that his whole life and what lay before him would set a precedent and would shape a new way of thinking for a paradigm shift in leadership, loyalty, honor, and commitment. He was right.

Here's a quote from George Washington to Catharine Sawbridge Macaulay Graham on January 9, 1790, about the destiny that George knew he would set for the American; presidency, family; community and social life.

"I walk on untrodden ground. There is scarcely any part of my conduct which may not hereafter be drawn into precedent."

Happiness, enjoyment, and character building is a journey in one's mind. Life may be harsh and unfair at times. Washington's life was harsh and inequitable (you'll see that in his educational journey).

This quote from George Washington to Mary Ball Washington (George's mother) on February 15, 1787, sums up the sculpture of character that George had in his time and culture. That we can have today in our culture. "Happiness depends more on the internal frame of a person's mind than on the externals in the world."

George Washington understood that a man's destiny is up to him, and his free will to choose despite the circumstances surrounding that individual.

Happiness is in a person's mind, not external circumstances. On December 5, 1790, in a letter to George's nephew, George Steptoe Washington, He said: "…a good moral character is first essential in a man…it is therefore highly imperative that you should endeavor not only to be learned but virtuous." So how do you build good character? Anyone can be calm, confident, or courageous. But how do you get that way but still retain your personality? Sometimes the world says you can't and fills you with fear of failure. But that same person has the choice to be weak, feeble or stagnate and fall into that fear. George Washington could have been fearful during the Seven Years War and not get his start in the battlefield as he did.

So how do you build a character that stays with you? There are a lot of questions that people think about when conversing about George Washington, and the main one was his character. He carried many traits with him, his whole life that he learned when he was just a boy. But he chose to act this way. People have a choice of their own free will to have the character of honor, prudence, loyalty, and chivalry that George had and learned from in his past errors and experience.

You could sum up experience in a quote from a George Washington letter to John Armstrong on March 26, 1781. "We ought not to look back, unless it is to derive useful lessons from past errors and for the purpose of profiting by dear bought experience, To enveigh against things that are past and irremediable, is unpleasing, but to steer clear of the shelves & rocks we have struck upon, is the part of wisdom, equally incumbent on political, as other men, who have their own little bark; or that of others to navigate through the intricate paths of life, or the trackless ocean to the haven of secury and rest."

People talk a lot about how George was. That's all they do is talk. Instead of putting those character traits into action. People have to practice it, and then those George Washington traits will become second nature.
People talk about loving your neighbor or getting better at a hobby. It's time to stop moping around like drips on a faucet and throw your shoulders back with confidence and do what you're called to do. Nobody can make you change into something. You have to choose to change when presented the information to be better, like this quote from George in a letter to Governor Robert Dinwiddie on August 27, 1757.

"It is with pleasure I receive reproof, when reproof is due, because no person can be readier to accuse me, than I am to acknowledge an error, when I am guilty of one; nor more desirous of atoning for a crime, when I am sensible of having committed it."

Nobody, when they are born, has a perfect character. It has to be built. And George Washington was the same way. He was born February 22, 1732, and passed away on December 14, 1799. From a young age, George was surrounded by rules, civility, and etiquette living in the Virginia countryside. His loving but firm mother, Mary Ball, instituted this way of life at a young age for George. His father Augustus passed away when George was only fourteen years old.

Furthermore, George learned about God and putting Him first along with schoolwork involving reading writing and arithmetic. Later in his childhood, young Washington would supposedly write down 110 maxims of civility. Lawrence, George's half brother, was someone that George looked up to. He admired Lawrence for his courage and adventurous life. Lawrence was part of the British Army and had quite the courageous, heroic experience that George craved. Young George enjoyed his visits to Mount Vernon between other family homes after the passing of his father, Augustus. Think about this, as a young person you are enamored by everything around you because it's new and exciting. You are a product of your environment, whether you like it or not. George Washington was no different. He was indubitably soaking up his atmosphere with Lawrence. It's not said, but you can imagine George learning a great deal about being a man and being a responsible adult who takes care of their business.

On a trip to Barbados that George accompanied Lawrence on, George came down with a case of smallpox that gave him immunity for the rest of his life. This international trip would be George's only trip outside of the continental United States.

Traveling to a different country and learning about a different culture and people, at a young age must have had a significant effect on Young George.

Terrible as that might be to come down with smallpox on a trip with your big brother, this turned out to be very beneficial for the grand divine plans in George's future. He must have gained some sense of mental strength going through an illness such as smallpox at a young age. The battlefield of life starts in your mind. And **your believing images of victory will take you as far as you want to go**. Continuing George's quest for character and adventure he attended school in 1745 in Fredericksburg Virginia, where it is said that he famously wrote down the rules of civility.

Some biographers of George Washington would beg to differ that he actually cared enough to write these rules down but instead was just doing a writing exercise. Either way, it's still a reasonable writing exercise of discipline, like Bart Simpson, writing at the beginning intro of the hit tv show "The Simpsons." George also had a plethora of books available to him from his family to educate himself as well on the moral character that he is globally known for today.

So what's the difference about whether George was doing a writing exercise or not? He cared about his education. He wanted to learn from his half brother Lawrence whom he admired. If you go to Mount Vernon and walk through where George's study is, you will see all the books he possessed for his personal education. Sounds better to me than watching the news.

A person can get the best education in the world from Harvard, Oxford, or Duke University. But it's up to the individual to apply those principles to grow into the men and women they want to become. A lot of people stop their education early in their life. You stay the same if you do that. And one might add that the more you care about your character and your education in whatever you desire, (not to say college is useless), the more successful you will be. Because the best school in the world doesn't mean anything unless you apply what you've learned with virtue and integrity. And a person's education may come from a variety of different resources. Bartholomew Dandridge was George's wife's nephew. And in a letter from George to Bartholomew in 1797, he said this regarding accomplishments and character. "Without Virtue and integrity, the nest talents of the most brilliant accomplishments can never gain the respect or conciliate the esteem of the precious part of mankind."

Everyone is born into different circumstances with different opportunities to grow or stay the same mentally. Life is not fair. But if we don't enjoy the situation that we are currently in, we can change it a little or a lot. For better or for worse. Like I said earlier, George's father passed away at a young age, which had a significant impact on him and what he was to do with his life. I'm sure many people reading this book who grew up or are growing up in a single-parent home or have adopted parents had possibly had some anxiety, condemnation or fear that young

When George was in his teen's, he had a missing parental figure. What kind of character did he have? George was all about self-education because of missed opportunities not available from his father. He was quietly ambitious about most things in his life. And his education was no different.

He never got to go to a well-known college. George's other brother went to Appleby College in England. But the opportunity for George to get a formal education had passed with the death of his father, Augustus. That's why George was so fascinated with learning for his knowledge that came from his family or his surveying opportunities and war. George always found a way to his goals. And his education was no different. You also have the ability as he did to educate yourself on seeking the truth. Not their truth or my truth but the truth on a matter of anything. He was going to the source to educate himself and build his sculpture of character.

George cared about his character. Do you care about your personality and how far it will take you? He never wanted to be stuck in a rut or stagnate. He most likely learned this from Lawrence. Yes, George was internally very ambitious. But you can't be determined and be lazy and stagnate at the same time.

 You will never get to your goal! And yes, there are times to decompress from life's tribulation and stress, but we shall not reap the benefits of good character if we faint not on our goals. We see George's ambition from his myriad of accomplishments. But he understood the importance of learning from his surroundings, his peers, and adversity's to be a better person for his family, friends, and colleagues.

Are you willing to have awkward conversations and move through things that may seem unpleasant in those few minutes? George brought things up to people appropriately as soon as he could to fix the problem or to make something better. Look up the situation surrounding the betrayal of Edmund Randolph during Washington's second term as President. George befriended and confided in a few colleagues like Hamilton and Lafayette, and De Steuben. They learned from him and vice versa. That's another way to self educate yourself. George learned a skilled trade, and had a military career, was an entrepreneur, was a politician and had a loving family. Sometimes in today's culture with the financial resources available to us, we can't get that formal education. But we can learn a trade, go into the military or have trial and error, and be an entrepreneur. As the world changes and college tuition goes up, some people won't be able to afford to go to college. But they can do what Washington did to self-educate themselves with a skilled trade or go into the military.

People have got to care about their character and education, or they will go nowhere in life. Look at George and the hurdles of losing his father and stepbrother at a young age.

That's devastating. But good character teaches us to deal with loss and move on to other things. To remember the good, forget the bad and preserver through the ugly. Think about your life and the damages you may have had? Did you sit back and waste time? Yes, there is a time to grieve, mourn, and reminisce. But sooner rather than later we have to grow up and move forward. That's what the people we have lost, (our loved ones and family), would have wanted. That is what Augustus Washington would have wished for George, to move forward and find a way to succeed! Because if you don't, you will always be stuck in a rut of despair.

Building good character means being a leader first of yourself and taking responsibility for your environment. Weak leaders will accomplish their goals because they have a vision or desire. But they lack the discipline, ambition, or training to become great. All leaders have some sort of imagination and passion. But the one thing that weak leaders lack that great leaders have is simple to achieve. The quality that George obtained from a lifetime of continuous learning is still influential today. Confidence, in yourself, and your dreams, desires, and goals are important to building good character. Confidence that is be admired is not haughty, shooting your mouth off. But being quick to listen and slow to speak. It's sometimes realizing you won't be right, but you can get better. George Washington never gave up on these ambitions.

George had a desire to go into the royal navy. But his mother Mary Ball had strong opinions for George to not go. She probably felt this way because Augustus had passed away on April 12, 1743, and didn't want to lose another family member, especially a child. Years later, when George was into his twenties, he picked up a trade in surveying. He was asked by Lord George William Fairfax, to do the surveying. George had a connection because his half-brother Lawrence had married a young Fairfax woman.

We can conclude that George was confident in his endeavors through the hurdles and opportunities of growth and through losses. George Washington always saw the opportunity for growth because he never let shaky, uncertain circumstances judge his character and attitude.

What about the doubt, worry and fear that lurks in one's mind because of what people say? George never let the opinions of others dictate his future. Sometimes things were not available in his life, and he had to regroup his thinking and plot another course of victory. He wanted to go into the royal navy, but instead, he became the commander and chief of the Continental Army. Washington still got to go into the military just in a different way. See what I mean about plotting a different course when things aren't available?

It takes strong courage to understand the word "no" and move forward to something greater, which more than likely has better benefits. Of course, everyone is afraid or worries at some point in their lives, but it's what you do with that worry or fear that makes you strong or weak. George could see and knew that many people looked up to him as his career and his family grew. So he tried his best to show people his calm demeanor, but deep inside, he was concerned about the outcome. How could you not be concerned with family or leading an army?

It takes an acute awareness of one's self to know that fear kills and poisons any goals. George had to be strong mentally in 1755 near the current location known as Pittsburgh in the battle of Monongahela when two horses were shots out from under him, and four bullet holes were shot through his clothes. But because of his ambition, character, and acute awareness of self. George kept calm during the battle of the French and Indian war. Sure he was scared, but a good leader is calm in their outward appearance despite the circumstances. A stellar book on leadership that I highly suggest is "Extreme Ownership: How U.S. Navy SEALs Lead and Win" by Jocko Willink and Leif Babin.

If you really want something in life, it's available to them that believe it can happen. You just have to position yourself in the right places, with the right people and have an ambitious attitude, just like George, because persistence does not need public approval.

In the most intense austere of circumstances where the emotions run high, and the smoke from musket fire was burning his eyes, he never wavered on the principles he was taught by his beloved but firm mother or the one hundred ten maxims he wrote down as a young boy.

George never had a formal education. Some people in our society don't get to go to school or college, ever. That's ok. You can still succeed in life just as George did.

We can choose to live in the doldrums of life, when life is condemning us to bad fortunes, or we can live and walk victoriously on the mountain of goal crushing, surrounding yourself with the right people who help us to be proactive, confident and assertive in our lives. George surrounded himself with people of strong personalities but people who weren't afraid to give George the truth to get to the desired goal of character or achievement. Rule number fifty-six in George Washington's rules of civility and decent behavior. "Associate yourself with men(people) of good quality if you a steam your own reputation for tis better to be alone than in bad company."

REAL FAKE NEWS

George Washington said to Joseph Reed on December 15, 1775, that " There's no restraining men's tongues or pens when charged with a little vanity."

Have you ever thought why all of a sudden from 2015 to 2016 there was this bastion of reporters and journalists putting out and talking about fake news stories? Propaganda and fake news has been around for thousands of years and did not originate with President Donald Trump. Yes, Donald Trump could indubitably afford to tweet a little less and say things a little more tactfully. But to President Trump's defense, in George Washington's first term in office "fake news" was roaring like a burning forest between Alexander Hamilton and Thomas Jefferson. Say what you will of Donald Trump and his tweeting but he gets his message out and cuts through the noise of the main stream media. I am sure that Washington would have loved to have tweeted whatever he was thinking during the Revolutionary War, Constitutional Convention, or at Mount Vernon and during his presidency. Both Jefferson and Hamilton as stated in Jack. D. Warren Jr's book, "The Presidency of George Washington," they vehemently disliked each other. This concocted an environment as slanderous as today's media.

George had great respect for both of these men. But frankly, they were acting like toddlers when they didn't get their way. Both of these men, Jefferson, and Hamilton had newspapers from staunch supporters of them, shoveling horrid nonsense and defamation slander against one another because of their opposing viewpoints of government. Jefferson's newspaper he used was called the "National Gazette" by Philip Freneau. Hamilton's newspaper was the "Gazette of the United States" by John Fenno.

One of George's most significant warnings or fears through-out his administration and time in public office was partisanship, (unknowingly Washington himself was a Federalist). People are not going to the person they have a problem with to solve the problem, it only builds the fire of resentment and division and spews the issue in the public eye of social media. Jefferson wanted to get away from the Federalist ideal of government intervention to a more Republican states rights kind of way of life. Whereas Hamilton preferred a more strong centralized Federal Government with reaching power to sustain the country through crises. Both of these men were intellectually geniuses of their times, but it was these two where we can find the seeds of party division that so many of us today despise. We are reminded of two things.

First a quote from George in 1790 "If we mean to support The Liberty and Independence which it has cost us so much blood and treasure to establish, we must drive far away from the demon of party spirit." If George Washington were alive today, he would prefer to avoid differences in political agendas within news reporting and for reporters and journalists to be in one accord or in one mind and just report the facts instead of opinion regardless of who wins elections.

Further education on fake news during George Washington's presidency can be found in the following books "The Presidency of George Washington" by Jack D. Warren, Jr on pages 61-73 "George Washington: The Wonder of the Age" by John Rhodehamelon pages 259-262 and in "His Excellency" by Joseph Ellis on pages 215-221.

Washington would absolutely not be ok with the party systems we have today. But George would have to get over the fact the people are always going to disagree and have political parties. He most likely would want people to have civility and chivalry without the defamation and slander during elections. George would be ok with comprising because that is how we got the founding documents that he fought for and signed.

YOU SET YOUR OWN DESTINY

What is the point in the Constitution of the United States? Why did the founders risk their lives, fortunes, and sacred honor for generations of Americans, they would never know?
George Washington understood that for a mixing melting pot of people to live together, they had to have a contract or binding resolution of how to coincide. They had to see the big picture and work together with each other's strength's ignoring the little things that annoyed them.
 George Washington would be absolutely disgusted with how we, as a country, have treated each other as citizens, humans, and residents of this country the last 200 years. George wanted badly to get married and did so around the age of 27 to Martha. But what about other people who want to get married today? Homosexuality or being gay was a crime back then. Whether people agree with the homosexual lifestyle or not, they have a right to do as they wish because of their free will and under the Constitution and the respective states in which they live.

The bill of rights was meant to guarantee rights to the citizenry without infringement from the Federal Government. And the rights that really protect a person's free will of the Constitution are the 9th and 10th amendments.

The 9th amendment to the U.S. Constitution states, "The enumeration in the Constitution, of certain rights, shall not be construed to deny or disparage others retained by the people."

And the 10th amendment says that "The powers not delegated to the United States by the Constitution, nor prohibited by it to the States, are reserved to the States respectively, or to the people." So what does this mean in relation to people of the same sex getting married? Would George Washington be accepting of homosexuals and same-sex marriage? Another salient educational source about the 9th and the 10th amendment can be shown in The Heritage Guide to the Constitution pages 366-375.

Well the 9th amendment essentially means in plain terms that "There are other rights within the constitution that have not been stated but should not be violated because the constitution would be really long if we wrote down everything" And 10th amendment essentially means that "any power that is not given to the federal government is given to the states or the people or the Constitution would be volumes and volumes long."

I mean for goodness sakes some congress members of today don't even read the entire bill. The 10th amendment solidifies the 9th amendment and Vise Versa. So then why does the Federal Government think they need to make federal laws about what marriage in President Clinton, Bush and Obama's administrations? It seems to me that it would be easier to manage and get the people within the state to agree or to disagree about same-sex marriage. Because getting about 325 million people, (about how many citizens live in the United States), to agree seems far more complicated than getting a state with a few million people to agree.

This does not mean, and it does not state in the Constitution that every state has to be the same in the laws they pass. If someone does not like the laws in which they live, they COULD POSSIBLY move to a different state. We have fifty of them plus a few U.S. territories to choose from. I mean, hell, if someone doesn't like what is happening in their state they can vote to change those state laws, or move to a different state. The beauty of the United States is the electric variety of states and demographics of culture.

People have a right to disagree if they choose to. If we were all the same and agreed on all the same topics, life would be completely uninteresting, and would become utterly boring. In this instance, it would stifle an avenue for innovation and creativity. Furthermore, people can disagree with the homosexual lifestyle, but that doesn't mean a person can't be friendly and kind to people they disagree with. You know the phrase "Treat others as you would want to be treated." That means people you disagree with too. Because if people are not friendly and kind, then why would they expect others to do that same for you? I want people to be nice and kind and hear me out. Everyone desires their colleagues, friends, family, neighbors, co-workers, and people they meet in public to be kind, chivalrous, and have civility towards them. It's OK that we don't agree on everything. If we were all the same, life would be monotonous. Variety gives spice to life. Furthermore, the Constitution states that the Legislative Branch makes the laws, not the Supreme Court. But the Supreme Court has the ability to make or have common law, which is the ability for the courts to establish law, based on previous cases of the court without violating the whole of the Constitution. The point of the Constitution is for all the strengths in the branches of government to work together to form a more perfect union. Meaning our country is not ever going to be perfect.

But each branch of government should stay in its lane and do its job. The fifty state governors and U.S. territories should have more ability to provide what their citizens need without violating federal law. Also, the three branches of the Federal Government should endeavor to keep or guard that unity in the spirit that is the essence of America.

The essences of what makes us great in America are the founding documents. Furthermore, The Federalist Papers that were written by Alexander Hamilton, (who was GW's figurative son and secretary of state in George's first term), and John Jay who was the first Chief Justice of the Supreme Court, and James Madison who later become the 4th president of the United States, helped to bolster the logic and reasoning for ratification of the Constitution.

These above-stated men, including George and many others, sought to help the states to work together and but be distinctly different. The 13 colonies all had their own ideas or ways of doing things in their region of the country in commerce, agriculture, or infrastructure.

Why did the Supreme Court's decision in a 2015 ruling, say all fifty states should let the LGBT community get married? The federal court decisions in 2015 about same-sex marriage seems like a violation of the 9th and 10th amendments and article one section 7 and 8 of the Constitution? The Congress didn't sign a bill into law, nor did the president sign an executive order.

The fifty state governments have different needs and may not want same-sex marriage in their state for various reasons, and they have a right to that because of the 9th and 10th amendments. If someone doesn't like what laws are in the state they reside, they can move to a different state that suits them best. Or bring that issue up in their state legislature. Or just agree to disagree and move on with their life. The point of having fifty different states is not for fifty utopian places to live. It is for fifty different dynamic, vivacious states and U.S. territories to attend to its citizens' needs. Did you know George Washington had a German general who was suspected homosexual in the beginning of the war and living in the military? His name was Baron de Steuben. Steuben was hired by Benjamin Franklin and Silas Deane then given to General Washington to help train the troops to shoot, march, organize, and keep the army hygienically clean during and after the paradigm-shifting events of Valley Forge. Steuben was a very interesting man. In Friedrich Kapp's biography in 1859 we see a man hungering for purpose! Steuben gets relieved out of his job in Europe and that community for speculated lifestyle habits of being a homosexual as stated in Paul Lockhart's book "The Drill Master of Valley Forge" on pages 39-42. Furthermore, Steuben would have been sent to jail if the Americans, namely Ben Franklin, didn't snatch up Steuben and take him to America. The Americans needed someone like Steuben to drill discipline and order into the soldiers, or the Cause was lost. On page 46 of Lockhart's book, it states that

"Hoping that Washington and Congress would simply forget about the specifics of his past." Steuben was in a hurry to get to Paris to leave for the Colonies but he forgot some important papers. The Americans desperately needed someone like Steuben to help procure the cause of liberty, so they did what they had to do to get Steuben to America.

Washington only needed Steuben's expertise in training the troops and battlefield experience. George didn't care a whole lot about a person's personal life unless it interfered with the goals of the country to free all the people in one way or another.

George knew that Steuben was a suspected homosexual. But Washington needed someone who was an expert to train the troops, or we surely would have lost the war and the Cause. All George simply required of people was loyalty to him, the cause and victory in war. He couldn't afford to let personal problems or lifestyles get in the way of the mission of freedom for all, at that time. If someone wouldn't or couldn't do something George would find a way to do it, or find someone who could do it for him, kind of like he did at the crossing of the Delaware River to attack the Hessians despite all that was against him. Think about this for a second, if George would have let Drill Master Steuben's lifestyle get in the way of training the troops like he was hired for, then we probably would have lost the war for lack of discipline and lack of hygienic environment in the army. Washington would have changed leadership. He didn't have time for anything else but victory. But Washington needed the best of the best. And Steuben was the very best. It doesn't matter what you do at home. But when you're at work, you work. That's why you're there. Steuben's work was to train and make ready the colonial troops for war.

So, back to 2015 in the court case called Obergefell v. Hodges. In the majority opinion of the high court, not once did they mention the nineth and tenth amendments. Even if we consider the 1996 "Defense Of Marriage Act" which is the opposite of the 2015 court decision, we still get some violation of the Constitution. Despite how you feel, you come to the Words of the Constitution unbiasedly for solutions. And the truth is that you can't get 325 million people to agree on everything. It is more manageable to decide things on the smaller state levels.

Can you even get everyone in your extended family to agree on everything? Good luck! Both times the pendulum swung to help same-sex couples and to disregard them. But what about the whole rest of the people in the other states to decide for themselves what's good for them that shall not be violated as a right? Isn't what the 9th and 10th amendments are for? Even if the 2015 court case is a good thing for gay couples why disregard a majority of the country who don't agree, just to suit a political agenda?

Letting each state decide takes more precise care of each citizen because there is a smaller microcosm to handle than the whole of the nation. The Federal Government has no right to tell the whole of the United States whom you should marry or not because that's a violation of the 9th and 10th amendments despite how you feel. The 2015 Supreme Court decision was a total disregard for two of the original amendments in the bill of rights.

The court cited the 14th amendment, among other things. The 1996 decision used the 5th amendment, which in essence disregarded the states who wished to recognize same-sex couples. Why such a forgetful memory of the 9th and 10th amendments unless it suits a political agenda?

For more information on this 2015 Supreme Court case see this link here: (www.britannica.com/event/Obergefell-v-Hodges).

So you can see from this short little chapter that decisions within the home of a family or the personal lifestyle choices that people make were not important to George as long as you did your job and were loyal to the Cause. He never took more seriously the importance of his family and of Martha his wife. That's the whole point in the idea of America. You free-will choice for you and your family. Steuben would have wanted to be left alone to his lifestyle if you look at his personal life.

These personal decisions we make in our lives are up to the states individually and to the people. Not the Federal Government who seeks only the power they which to keep. Whether people agree or not with homosexuality and same-sex marriage is a different topic. But this chapter was written to highlight the freedoms we have in the Constitution as a whole, and not nitpick political agenda we would like to see passed. There are about 325 million people in the United States. Not everyone is going to agree. But getting a state of about 11 million people would be a lot easier to pass a bill through a state legislature. The only reason why the Supreme Court made that law in 2015 is that Congress would have never passed that bill into law, which is very sneaky and smart because it would have violated states rights.

What about the popular cultural and political agendas to make recreational marijuana legal? As far as I can tell, there is no evidence that George Washington smoked marijuana of any kind. He grew hemp for industrial uses like for rope and canvas sacks but not for getting high. Even though people may disagree with marijuana or drug use, that is a right up to the states to decide what people do, not the Federal Government. And I would again point people towards the 9th and 10th amendments.

To conclude this chapter, I would point you to "First Entrepreneur" by Edward Lengel pages 60 & 69 and this link (www.mountvernon.org/george-washington/facts/george-washington-grew-hemp) on MountVernon.org about Washington and his industrial use of hemp.

FAMILY AND FRIENDS

What do you consider a true friend? Have you ever thought about what the near perfect spouse would be like? George Washington was a true friend to many.

Some people he encountered, whom he befriended he, had many differences of opinion like Thomas Jefferson, who left his cabinet in the first term of Washington's presidency. He was loyal to a fault at times and always thought the best of people. Doesn't that sound like a good companion? What would you consider a good friend to be? People who always pander to you and don't tell you the truth will never help you grow.

Washington wanted to be surrounded by the most intellectual and astute people of his time like James Madison, (who wrote the U.S. Constitution) and Thomas Jefferson who wrote the Declaration of Independence or even Baron de Steuben. Washington knew he did not know it all. He was just confident in what he did know. Washington disagreed with his colleagues at times, but that doesn't mean you give up right away on your friends or your family or people you work with. You fight for that relationship in a harmonious way.

A good friend, like George, confided in and persevered through the toughest times with his companions. Switching gears to parenting, I am not currently a parent but logically to me, if two people are going to conceive and bring a new breathing life into the world and take responsibility for it, (traditionally speaking), why then do we have many babies born out of wedlock? Seems to me that people didn't think of the consequences of their actions. Remember we have the God-given free will to choose our own destiny. But we are not free from the consequences of our choices, whether good, bad or indifferent.

So if you have a child out of wedlock and are frustrated or upset about it that was your choice to do so, and you must live with those choices you make. The notion that parents shouldn't direct a child's steps or take care of the child they conceived is a misnomer and foolish. Why would you let social media, societal norms, movies, music and anything else the world propagates, parent your children, that you wish your child not to be exposed to at a young age? George and Martha Washington took especially acute care of Washy and Nelly, the children from Martha's first marriage. Even though they never had children of their own.

What did you think was going to happen after sex if you're not careful and protect yourself? Children would be your responsibility if you chose to have them, to raise those kids as you see appropriate. You are totally responsible for everything that the child learns and does at a young age. George and Martha were responsible for the children they cared for and raised. You have free will. Not all children are going to grow up to be what the parents want them to be. And that's ok. Look at George Washington's life. He ended up going into the military anyway even though Mary Ball Washington pleaded that he not go. He found another way to his military goal, and he became commander of the Continental Army. Mary Ball was honest, and that's all that parents and friends can be to help and guide those in their lives. We can't control people when they become adults because we have free will. But honesty goes a lot further to feed relationships than dishonesty does. Parents should be honest with their kids. Just think what would have happened to the colonies if George didn't obey his mother and went into the royal navy? George most likely would not have been our president or as involved in the formation of the United States. And yes I'll admit Mary Ball was strict, but she was fair. Think about what you would do if you had children? Would you act as Mary Ball did and forbid your child to go on an adventure because something inside your conscious is telling you to try to save your child's life? I think that's pretty appropriate for George's situation. Martha Washington was another influential person in George's life. Martha was the most pivotal individual in George's life. She helped refine George's strength and confidence in front of people. She took care of Mount Vernon and their family while George was away to take on the world. Martha was very strong, beautiful, and wise. Even though this "Queen of Virginia" as I like to say had lots of financial backing and could pick any man to marry, she chose the quiet and chivalrous George Washington. Her presence demanded respect because of her confidence as an individual, and a woman, and her husband, who's name commanded respect from taking on the whole world. She could handle tense situations at Mount Vernon and know what her husband George would want.

They were a team and inseparable from the beginning. And being dating being engaged or married means you communicate honestly, kindly and salted with commitment just like George and Martha did. Martha was there in camp with George in just about half of the battles he was a part of. George loved no one more honestly and truly than Martha. George had a few uttering infatuations before he married Martha at twenty-six. But Martha was the one for him. She was his absolute confidant and best friend. We could learn a thing or two about how to treat women and others from George. I believe that our world would be a lot friendlier and we'd have more harmonious friendships, relationships, and acquaintances if we did as George did. George suffered from many ailments and physical challenges. There is no way on God's green earth that this man could have taken on the world with the measles, dysentery, dental issues, malaria, smallpox, melanoma and other ailments without the loving tender care of his beloved Martha. Also, there is no record of Martha and George arguing. And Martha burned most of the letters between her and George after his passing. But shouldn't the things that are between a family or a couple remain private?

Would you want everyone knowing your business? George and Martha loved to entertain, host, and dance but they kept the confidant conversations between them and them alone. George Washington once said to Bushrod Washington on January 15, 1783 "...Be courteous to all, but intimate with few, and let those few be well tried before you give them your confidence? True friendship is a plant of slow growth, and must undergo and withstand the shocks of adversity before it is entitled to the appellation." This stands true today in the realm of relationships of all kinds, whether its dating, friends, or co-workers. Think about how many times you have poured your heart out only to get it stepped on. George Washington had many times in his life like that. Benedict Arnold for one, deeply hurt Washington in 1780 because he tried to give West Point over to the British. Washington was Arnold's "good friend." But Arnold had other intentions and let his pride get the best of him. It's ok to be honest with people because that is what people need to grow. You can't be friends or married to someone who is continually dishonest. That relationship is doomed to fail like Benedict, and George's was.

In Glenn Beck's book "Being George Washington" on pages 81-113 gives a better pictorial view of the emotional turmoil that George went through in finding out about Arnold's betrayal. Iron sharpens iron, and so a friend sharpens the countenance of his friends. We can't be true friends with everyone we meet, but we can have civility for a more harmonious life.

If someone is not helping, challenging or giving (not necessarily monetarily) to you, then George Washington would tell you to probably rethink that confidence you have in that so-called acquaintance or friend. Remember you don't have to take all the advice from your friends, you just have to listen. That's what George would do. It takes time, patience, kindness, and honesty to develop a strong, long-lasting friendship. Not everyone you meet is going to be your friend. Not everyone you meet is going to be kind or generous to you. Having a small tiny circle of time trusted friends is wise. George did. He had Martha, Alexander Hamilton, Henry Knox, Billy Lee, Marquis de Lafayette and Friedrich Wilhelm von Steuben among a few others that had Washington's full support and trust.

MILITARY

Funding/Preparation/Mindset

Have you ever thought about what it would be like to not have the proper shoes or clothes? What about being in a medical situation without the proper tools or information to understand what is going on with your medical needs? Have you been in a circumstance where your transportation or education was uncertain? I've used the word salient a lot in this short book. But I want to get straight to the facts and not beat around the bush. Here is some straight to the facts quotes about George Washington and military funding, preparation, and mindset of the military.

George once said during his First annual address to Congress on January 8, 1790 "To be prepared for war is one of the most effectual means of preserving peace."

He also said on his 5th Annual address to Congress on December 13, 1793 that: "If we desire to avoid insult, we must be able to repel it; if we desire to secure peace, one of the most powerful instruments of our rising prosperity, it must be known, that we are at all times ready..."

And finally, Washington said early in his military career to the Virginia Regiment on January 8, 1756. "Remember that it is the actions, and not the commission, that make the officer, and that there is more expected from him, than the title."

George Washington was in many situations where he was cut short in financial backing or new technology to procure a battle or health of the army and troops during the Revolutionary War. Thousands of soldiers died from weather conditions or disease. During the time of Valley Forge and the crossing the Delaware River to conquer the Hessians, the colonial troops lacked basic items like proper shoes, clothes, and blankets. But through all of this, how did the troops that remained and The General commanding the Continental Army stay the course? They believed in the Cause.

The soldiers believed that fighting for freedom, and planting seeds of freedom so all people could be free, was worthy of their bloodshed. Washington did more than just command troops on the battlefield.

In essence, General Washington commanded their hearts and lives to the destiny of being remembered for the ones who procured freedom for the cause of liberty. Washington essentially invented the C.I.A. before it was even a thought in the 20th century.

Washington put together the Culper spy ring and help defeat the British through disinformation and deliberately deceiving the enemy to win. If it weren't for this group of six brave people and Washington, the outcome of the war would absolutely have been different. Washington had little funds and had to think outside the box to win. To do just that he deliberately deceived the enemy.

On many occasions, Washington wrote to Congress to fund the basic necessities of the war. Even though the continental army didn't have the finances or innovation to fight the war, Washington was a genius when it came thinking ahead. His ultimate plan was to outlast the British and tire them out by outmaneuvering them. Washington was a surveyor, so he understood the landscape of the colonial land. With his knowledge of the landscape, he knew he could outsmart and outmaneuver the British. Many times Washington lost a battle, but he kept fighting on because he knew what he was doing was right and just.

For example, George Washington wrote to Lieutenant Colonel John Laurens on January 15, 1781, about the embarrassment of the financial aspect of the war. Washington was fully aware that something needed to be done.

George went on to say "..secondly that, notwithstanding from the confusion, always attendant on a revolution, from our having had governments to frame, and every species of civil and military institution to create; from that inexperience in affairs, necessarily incident to a nation in its commencement, some errors may have been committed in the administration of our finances, to which a part of our embarrassments are to be attributed, yet they are principally to be ascribed to an essential defect of means, to the want of a sufficient stock of wealth, as mentioned in the rest article; which, continuing to operate, will make it impossible, by any merely interior exertions, to extricate ourselves from those embarrassments, restore public credit, and furnish the funds required for the support of the war."

Washington understood that the need for more financial support from Congress was important in winning the war and procuring the Cause. Washington, more than anyone else knew that the troops would have to be paid what was due them for their service or a mutiny could arise. You can see this in several letters General Washington wrote to Joseph Reed on December 15, 1775, and on March of 1783 and on June 14, 1783. The mutiny that never was, Washington pleaded with the soldiers in Newburgh New York about the pay that was due to them.

Congress stopped short of declaring war on its own army from an oncoming mutiny that General Washington squashed. How could you blame the soldiers for being upset? They were paid very little or nothing at all for their service to the infant country, to the cause that burned in their bones. Imagine if Congress ran out of finances to fund our military today? We would have a much bigger problem than a few thousand or so troops marching on the Capitol steps in Washington, D.C. We couldn't protect our cybersecurity, borders, or U.S territories if we ran out of money. No president in the last 243 years could have prevented a mutiny of the military like George Washington did. Not one president that we have had is more respected and honored, then George Washington. I understand that some politicians of today are willing to give little or next to nothing to the military. But if President Washington were alive today, he would absolutely support the total funding of the military and intelligence agencies. Yes, I believe that President Washington would update the military at any expense, for the duration of the war at hand, but not to exceed a proposed budget and especially fund basic necessities like shoes, blankets, and food. The soldiers had pretty much next to nothing when they deserved everything for their service.

If Washington were going, to sum up, the military of today, he possibly would refer back to his letter of instructions to the Captains of the Virginia Regiments on July 29, 1759. "Discipline is the soul of an army. It makes small numbers formidable; procures success to the weak, and esteem to all."

And also this quote to the first annual address to Congress on January 8, 1790: "To be prepared for war is one of the most effectual means of preserving peace."

Washington would agree with the modern military theory of peace through strength.

WORRY ABOUT YOURSELF FIRST

Many people have said that Washington's world view on isolationism is narrowminded, but think about what the world was like back in George's day? They did not have planes, the internet, or even telephones to communicate more efficiently. But in today's culture, we do have those things and much more. Our world is set on a global market, and we can't ignore our neighbors or what's happening across the Atlantic or to the north of the United States. It's ok to be cautious. I'm sure those of you fathers or mothers worry from time to time about your kids. Well, George Washington, who was the Father of this country, worried a little about us today. In John Avlon's book about Washington's Farewell, he talks of JFK who revered good ol George and JFK's rendition of George's farewell address.

JFK said "(George) told our forefathers to reject permanent, inveterate antipathies against particular nations and passionate attachments for others, and said a nation failing in this to some degree a slave. He warned against foreign influences which seek to tamper with domestic factions, who practice the arts of seduction, to mislead public opinion.

His rule for commercial relations was to have with them as little political connection as possible." (Avlon pages 270,271).

You can see that even a president such as JFK, many years after George, understood what George was saying. There is something good about putting America first, domestically and internationally and putting others second. How can we take care of other countries if we can't take care of ourselves as a country?

If there were two things that George would not be at peace with in the United States, it would be trading on global markets and alliances with other countries. On the topic of trade and the circumstance of the "Jay Treaty," George Washington's administration had successfully negotiated a quasi-good deal for both parties. The Jay Treaty was not perfect, but it solved the problem for the time being. It was a band-aid. There were many in the country who did not agree with Washington, but he did what he could to avoid another war with a powerful European country. A bad deal as I'm sure you know, is one where either participant doesn't feel satisfied or is not compensated enough after the deal is agreed upon.

The Jay Treaty essentially put us on a level playing field with the British.

What the treaty did was to withdraw British troops back behind the Canadian border, limit the bargaining of trade in the British East and West Indies and have a trade relationship where both counties would have favorable tariffs toward each other. The British realized they couldn't defeat us, so they decided to work with us. What a novel idea! What if counties of today in the eastern and western hemisphere thought like that? I'm sure there would be less war in the middle east like the Israel and Palestinian conflict if countries would comprise and not terrorize. Israel tried to make peace five times over the decades and Palestine stubbornly won't compromise. George's view of an America first policy back then is just as important now to take care of the ever-growing needs of our country today. If the politicians in Congress want the United States to shovel money to other countries, then we must learn to live within our means and save our money to a desired goal. If American families have to live that way, then the Federal Government should as well. Because if we had spread ourselves so thin back in George Washington's time and culture without strengthening our borders, our national security and our economy then we, (the United States), probably would have only lasted as a country for a hundred years or less in my opinion. If the United States contributes about 22% of the financial backing to the United Nations and the headquarters of the UN is inside the United States, then why does the United States have a tainted view from other countries within the United Nations? It's because some counties see the USA as a bully, (at times yes we've done horrible things) or maybe it's because of the jealousy in us being a superpower.

But think of George's isolationism like this; if you can't take of your own basic need first and develop a plan on improvement when times get tough, then how would we expect to take care of other countries or be apart of other world organizations that have more needs and bigger issues? The United States is not perfect, but the bondage that the United Nations brings is intolerable to a nation that gives so much to the rest of the world. One question that I know George would ask is what long term benefits does this alliance with the United Nations have for us, and what are the long term effects of the headquarters being on our soil? As you read this know that the United States did not start out to be the parents, police, or guardians of the world. And as it is said in the Spiderman comics "With great power comes great responsibility."

I believe Washington would most agree with President Trump on a few things about the United Nations and how they view us as the world superpower and trade in the global market.

Not much is known about what Washington would think about immigration. So we can not say or pontificate one ideology or another about this topic and Washington. But in his Farewell Address on September 19th, 1796 President Washington said "Citizens by birth or choice, of a common country, that country has a right to concentrate your affections. The name of AMERICAN, which belongs to you, in your national capacity, must always exalt the just pride of Patriotism, more than any appellation derived from local discriminations."

Also in a letter to vice president John Adams on November 15th 1794 Washington wrote;

"My opinion with respect to emigration is, that except of useful mechanic' s — and some particular descriptions of men — or professions — there is no need for extra encouragement: while the policy or advantage of its taking place in a body (I mean the settling of them in a body) may be much questioned; for by so doing they retain the language, habits & principles (good or bad) which they bring with them; whereas, by an intermixture with our people, they, or their descendants, get assimilated to our customs, manners, and laws: in a word, soon become one people."

Furthermore Washington wrote to Francis Adrian Van Der Kemp on May 28th, 1788 on the topic of immigration; "I had always hoped that this land might become a safe & agreeable Asylum to the virtuous & persecuted part of mankind, to whatever nation they might belong."

What would George Washington think about socialism? I don't know what he would think of socialism or communism today, but what we do know is that he and the Founding Father's looked back at the other types of governments to see what worked and what didn't.

What they came up with was a new form of government that has lasted through a civil war and two world wars and is still beating today. The Founding Fathers didn't revolt from the British government to get more of the same. They understood that taxes were necessary at times. And that government intervention (Whiskey Rebellion) is also necessary at times. Beyond that, I don't know what to say except here are some salient George Washington quotes about wisdom, experience in the context of America learning from other countries as well as our mistakes.

Edward Lengel, a Washington historian, said in his book called "First Entrepreneur" on page 249 that "In a free society no man can dictate how an economy functions. George Washington never had the power or the desire to do so. Neither as general nor as president did he command prosperity. Men of talent working alongside him-some lifelong friends and some, alas, eventual enemies-contributed vitally to winning the Revolutionary War fashioning a constitution creating a government and setting the nations course."

Yes, Washington was an entrepreneur. YOU can and have the ability to be an entrepreneur as well. Find a niche as he did. What do you think he would say about business?

In his correspondences to James Anderson on December 21, 1797, he said "System in all things is the soul of business. To deliberate maturely, & execute promptly is the way to conduct it to advantage. With me, it has always been a maxim, rather let my designs appear from my works, than by my expressions."

And this quote from George Washington to George Washington Parke Custis on January 07, 1798.

"I shall expect you will confide yourself to your studies, and diligently attend to them; endeavoring to make yourself master of whatever is recommended to, or required of you.

The hours allotted for study, if really applied to it, instead of running up & down stairs, & wasted in conversation with any one who will talk with you, will enable you to make considerable progress in whatsoever line is marked out for you: and that you may do it, is my sincere wish."

These two quotes could be something to think about with having the tenacity to start a business or find a niche like George once did. Or take care of your business and personal life like George did. From George Washington to the Society of Quakers, October 13, 1789, George said "Government being, among other purposes, instituted to protect the Persons and Consciences of men from oppression, it certainly is the duty of Rulers, not only to abstain from it themselves but according to their Stations, to prevent it in others."

Also In George's letter to Bushrod Washington, his nephew, on November 10, 1787 he said "If we cannot learn wisdom from experience, it is hard to say where it is to be found."

Furthermore in George's letter to Henry Lee, on *Oct. 31st, 1786 he said;* "Let the reins of government then be braced and held with a steady hand, and every violation of the constitution be reprehended. If defective, let it be amended, but not suffered to be trampled upon whilst it has an existence."

Also in a Washington letter to David Stuart, July 1, 1787 he said "No doubt there will be a diversity of sentiments on this important subject; and to inform the judgment, it is necessary to hear all arguments that can be advanced. To please all is impossible, and to attempt it would be vain. The only way, therefore, is, under all the views in which it can be placed, and with a due consideration to circumstances, habits, &c., &c., to form such a government as will bear the scrutinizing eye of criticism, and trust it to the good sense and patriotism of the people to carry it into effect. Demagogues, men who are unwilling to lose any of their State consequence, and interested characters in each, will oppose any general government. But let these be regarded rightly, and justice, it is to be hoped, will at length prevail."

In addition on the topic of government and The Constitution, Washington said to Benjamin Harrison on the 24th of September 1787 "I wish the constitution, which is offered, had been made more perfect; but I sincerely believe it is the best that could be obtained at this time. And, as a constitutional door is opened for amendment hereafter, the adoption of it, under the present circumstances of the Union, is, in my opinion, desirable."

President Washington would be cautious to join a new world order to give ultimate power to a singular global organization speaking for the hundreds of languages and billions of people on the earth. One could conclude based on these George Washington quotes that he would want some type of security at all of our borders and some type of assimilation of immigrants to our country. We could conclude that he would most likely put America's interest first rather than a global organization. In the 1700's people were traveling all over the world; it might not have been as technologically advanced, but it was global. What that looks like, I don't know. We must go solely off of George Washington's correspondence, speeches, and actions while he served as our first president to the United States.

RELIGIOUS TOLERATION

Washington was very tolerant of many things.
George understood the heavy pendulum balance
in which he was granted by the Almighty. And
Washington knew at times; mankind may act
indecently. But of everything in this world, what
is the one thing that holds a man's moral
compass and free will? It's God and God's Word.
Whether people believe in Christianity, Taoism,
or Islam, it's God's Word that sets people free
and sharpens the tone for mankind to live like a
two-edged sword. And mankind can choose to
listen to whatever God they desire as best they
can or completely disregard it. But beyond God
and His Word, how do you resolve conflict
without speaking about something so personal?
You have to have the tolerance for hearing
someone out and respectfully disagree for a
harmonious outcome.

George Washington believed in God and grew
up in a godly environment. His mother Mary
Ball and his father Augustus were godly people,
and George's great-great-grandfather was an
Anglican pastor. God and the Bible were very
vital throughout all of George Washington's life.

It's been recorded and documented that he went to church services throughout his life, especially during his presidency and that he prayed daily and even fervently, especially during the American Revolutionary War.

Now whatever lay in Washington's heart and whatever his true personal relationship with God was, he knew that God was important. He understood that God or believing in a godly sense, whatever people want to believe for their spirituality, is important to a person's vital health as a human. He understood that, as well as our other Founding Father's did. You can see that in our founding documents "endowed by their creator" and "certain unalienable rights", the 1st amendment in the Constitution is the freedom to believe in whatever you choose to believe in. Washington knew, and he came to believe that he was chosen by God for a purpose. You see that in the French and Indian war when Washington was shot at, had bullet holes through his coat and he had horses shot out from under him and he came out unscathed. George was a Freemason, and in that, there was an element of spirituality. For today in current culture, some people don't believe in God. The Word of God isn't for the unbeliever plain and simple. It is for the believer.

A well known leading atheist in America or in the world in a documentary was being interviewed by Ben Stein. That atheist's name is Richard Dawkins. The documentary is called "Expelled: no intelligence allowed." At the end of the documentary, Richard Dawkins talks about that we most likely came from an intelligent design of some kind.

Washington knew that spirituality was not to be taken lightly. You can see that in the many correspondences in his life and speeches he wrote. George most likely was Angelicin Christian. That is not totally proven. We can't really put a concrete depiction on what he really believed or what denomination he was, but it was most likely Angelicin. In today's concerning culture, you know the Word of God and however people worship God is for the believer, not the unbeliever. Doesn't that seem logical? If you disagree with that statement, then skip to the next chapter.

If George Washington were alive today, he would want and desire for people to have a spiritual relationship with God.

A spiritual relationship with God is the only thing that can truly fill a person's heart, that the Federal Government tries to fill.

Morality and virtue come from where? They certainly don't come from the Federal Government. Morality and virtue come from a belief in God. I'm trying to be vague here because I'm not trying to put one godly belief over another I'm just trying to just state the salient facts about George Washington.

No one else in the world understood the vital importance of tolerance more than George Washington. His mother Mary Ball was religious. I would say that George was very godly but not religious. He couldn't be religious. He had to separate his feelings from his responsibility of being the most-watched, admired, and scrutinized leader in the whole world. If Washington did not set the proper wavelength for religious tolerance, then that is another thing that very well may have torn our infant country apart from the very beginning.

In August 1790 Washington wrote to the Hebrew Congregation in Newport Rhode Island on thankfulness for their support and religious tolerance.

During the conclusion of the letter, he wrote "It is now no more that toleration is spoken of as if it were the indulgence of one class of people that another enjoyed the exercise of their inherent natural rights, for, happily the government of the United States, which gives bigotry no sanction, to persecution no assistance, requires only that they who live under its protection should demean themselves as good citizens in giving it on all occasions their effectual support". Washington's letter distinctly agrees with the current culture of being tolerant of all peoples beliefs (W.B. Allen pages 547-548). Washington understood God, and he understood that to put God first as the country's first leader, he had to be full of grace and mercy even of people's beliefs and decisions. He knew that as he was more tolerant, then the rest of the country, he had to be as well because the whole world was waiting for him to drop the hat. And they still are. George knew he needed to back his words up with his deeds. All of these things can be seen and recognized in President Washington's first inaugural address.

During his first inaugural address, President Washington stated:

"No People can be bound to acknowledge and adore the invisible hand, which conducts the Affairs of men more than the People of the United States. Every step, by which they have advanced to the character of an independent nation, seems to have been distinguished by some token of providential agency. And in the important revolution just accomplished in the system of their United Government, the tranquil deliberations and voluntary consent of so many distinct communities, from which the event has resulted, cannot be compared with the means by which most Governments have been established, without some return of pious gratitude along with an humble anticipation of the future blessings which the past seem to presage. These reflections, arising out of the present crisis, have forced themselves too strongly on my mind to be suppressed. You will join with me I trust in thinking, that there are none under the influence of which, the proceedings of a new and free Government can more auspiciously commence." George Washington took the reins of our country with firm hands, a sharp sword and tender words. He guided our country at its most important time, at its birth. Without George paving the way for our religious tolerance and understanding, our country very well may have been torn apart at its first steps as an infant nation.

HOLDING BACK THE TIDE

On August 15, 2017, President Donald Trump made a speech on the topic of the Charlottesville, Virginia protest that turned into rioting, and it's aftermath. Both sides were there to protest things that they believe to be true. To put it simply, one side of the protesters were there to protest the taking down of a Robert E. Lee statue and the other side wanted to protest an objection to that statue being taken down. Both sides at one point during the protest became violent like heathens in a burning fire.

During Trump's speech, he spoke about the events that unfolded, and as the president, he wished to get all the facts before saying something.

Wouldn't you want to get all the facts before speaking about a sensitive situation, especially if you were the leader of a country? President Trump eluded to the fact that he knew his words bring weight to any situation that's delicate or paramount (even though sometimes he tweets too much). Also President Trump made the point that George Washington, was a slave owner and asked the audience who were the press, if we as a country are going to take away George Washington's status and statues along with Robert E. Lee's?

Trump challenged the audience to consider whether they would remove all memory of former slave owners, even someone as monumental to the United States as George Washington. The reporters didn't know what to say to President Trump and were unable to address this challenge.

Before we get started on the topic of slavery, racial discrimination, and political bias, let me ask you a few questions…why did the reporters toss President Trump's challenge to the side? What was their motive? Did they understand what was being asked of them? What do you know about President George Washington and why don't people seem to talk about George anymore? What do you think George Washington would say to our country and what more can we do on this topic of race to simmer down the situation and move forward together? Yes, there is a lot of information and history about this topic. For the brevity of time, in keeping your attention, we will look at an overview on this topic of race and George Washington, but not forgetting the good, the bad and in the whole history of America. If our country is to move past this stain on American history, in the aspect of learning from our mistakes, what else is there to do?

Washington, like many sensible people of the day thought slavery was "immoral, but he owned slaves and rebuffed suggestions during his lifetime that he free them as an example to others. In Washington's will, however, he finally did so".(Kidder & Oppenheim page 162) Washington understood that for the founders, to call themselves free from tyranny, they had to plant the seeds to abolish slavery in the documents that would hold the country together through blood, sacrifice, and compromise. In our current culture some people want you to think that George didn't want to free his slaves and that he was racist. Have you ever thought of the context of that 1700's culture and the Constitution? Over George Washington's life, he understood that all Americans born here or who come here deserve to be free from involuntary servitude or slavery. George was also a product of his environment like all of us are. He was awed to think early in his adult life that slavery was acceptable. As he grew older, his mind began to change. And he knew as well as anyone else that it would take time.

There are notes from Thomas Jefferson which states in 1775 when George was talking to Edmond Randolph that if "The hypothesis of a separation of the Union into Northern and Southern said he had made up his mind to remove and be of the Northern." This, as you learn about George, was a comment made by a man not knowing what destiny awaits him on the battlefield and perhaps a foretelling of the Civil War. But if it weren't for the Founders and the documents that guaranteed absolute freedom then, slavery very well could have lasted into the 20th to 21st centuries.

Deep down it was up to George to turn the tide, to change a way of life and up-end a whole entire subculture of oppression for the United States to really be free.

George signed the Slave Trade act of 1794, which limited the U.S. involvement in the international slave trade. George and many other Founding Fathers knew and believed in a gradual abolishment of slavery.

If the Framers of the Constitution tried to tackle every single issue plaguing the newly founded country, they very well would not have agreed on anything or even finished the Constitution. We very well would have not had a country if the Founders decided to tackle every single issue, including slavery.

No matter who you talk to in the world who know about George, all they really say was that he was a great man. It was George who had the final say to make hard choices to keep the Union and solidarity of the United States together unless it is torn apart by un-natural unforgiving forces. Let's look at some fact's about our founding documents, and amendments to our Constitution and current events to see if there really is need to call for the continuous tidal wave of racism as a whole and if we can do anything NOW that relates to the founders of our country?

First, let us look at the Constitution and the Declaration of Independence and what the Framers really thought. George Washington was a man of honor and stood by his words with his deeds and he stood by his signing of the Constitution, though it was not perfect. On September 19, 1796, George Washington said this of the Constitution during his Farewell Address. "It is important…that the habits of thinking in a free country should inspire caution in those entrusted with its administration to connect themselves within their respective Constitutional spheres;…"
At the time of Martha's death, George freed his slaves according to his will. Even though he had already died few years earlier.

He stood by the Declaration of Independence and put pen to paper and signed his honor to the Constitution. So what about the 3/5 compromise in Article 1, Section 2 of the Constitution?

"Representatives…shall be apportioned among the… States by adding to the whole Number of free Persons... three-fifths of all other Persons." The Constitution does not say a slave person is not a physical human being or is property; it unequivocally says that they are "persons." A whole physical person. So why do people take things out of context? It's for political reasons or agendas. If the Founders wanted to talk about 3/5 of a physical person, they would have. This section of the Constitution is about population representation in Congress.
We are talking about the representation of people, not pets or property of any kind. We just read what the word or the truth says in The Constitution. That's it; there is no guessing here. Also, it does not say that a slave is three-fifths of a physical human person. Sometimes in life, if you don't know, say you don't know as not to look like a fool later. The "three-fifths" explanation had nothing to do with the real human value of an individual person in servitude but had absolutely wholly to do with how many representatives each State would have in the United States Congress.

Dr. Carol Swain, a former professor of political science, has a PragerU video and uniquely depicts the 3/5 compromise in a concise way to understand the intent and compromise of the slaveholders of the South and abolitionist of the North.

Dr. Swain states: "The three-fifths compromise was devised by those who opposed slavery, not by those who were for slavery. Or, to put it another way, it wasn't the racists of the South who wanted to count slave populations less than white populations – it was the abolitionists of the North. The framers of the Constitution were deeply divided on the issue of slavery. The free states of the North wanted to abolish it. The slave states of the South wanted to expand it. You might say that the southern slave states wanted to have it both ways: They wanted to count their slaves for the purpose of representation, but they didn't want to give any representation to their slaves. Why did this matter? Let's look at the numbers. In the 1790 census, just three years after the Constitution was ratified, the free states of New Hampshire, Massachusetts, Rhode Island, Connecticut, New York, New Jersey, Pennsylvania, and Delaware had a population of about 1.8 million free whites.The slave states of Maryland, Virginia, North Carolina, South Carolina, and Georgia, had about 1.1 million free whites, and 633,000 slaves. Add those two numbers, and you get nearly equal populations between the North and the South. By the time of the Civil War, the slave population had grown to 4 million. Imagine how much more powerful slave states would have been without the three-fifths compromise: If one hundred percent of the slave population had been counted, slavery may very well have lasted into the 20th century. Why you might ask, didn't the North simply insist that the South not count slaves at all? Because the slave states would never have agreed to join the Union. They would have formed their own country, and we would have had two nations— one free and one slave— living side-by-side in conflict from the very start. The three-fifths compromise was the solution to the most difficult challenge the Framers faced: how to create a single country out of people so divided on a fundamental issue. As discordant as the compromise sounds to modern ears, without it, there would have been no United States."

If we as a nation would have counted all enslaved peoples, the slave states would have had a majority in Congress with regards to representation and slavery very well would have lasted into the 1900s. 3/5 of the slave population was the compromise. Not 3/5 of a physical person compromise. So what have we learned? We have learned that George Washington must have known about the 3/5 compromise because he signed the Constitution. But what about the deleted passage from the Declaration of Independence against slavery? Thomas Jefferson was tasked with drafting the Declaration of Independence. This Declaration was essentially a letter to the king of England. And Jefferson knew that the king would stop at nothing unless the founders put it all in the table.

So here's the deleted passage of the Declaration of Independence about slavery;

"He has waged cruel war against human nature itself, violating its most sacred rights of life and liberty in the persons of a distant people who never offended him, captivating & carrying them into slavery in another hemisphere or to incur miserable death in their transportation thither. This piratical warfare, the opprobrium of indel powers, is the warfare of the Christian King of Great Britain.

Determined to keep open a market where Men should be bought & sold, he has prostituted his negative for suppressing every legislative attempt to prohibit or restrain this execrable commerce. And that this assemblage of horrors might want no fact of distinguished die, he is now exciting those very people to rise in arms among us, and to purchase that liberty of which he has deprived them, by murdering the people on whom he has obtruded them: thus paying o former crimes committed again the Liberties of one people, with crimes which he urges them to commit against the lives of another."

This passage of the Declaration of Independence that was left out was due to the states of Georgia and South Carolina who heavily supported the institution of slavery. The thirteen colonies knew that for this grand experiment of forging a nation to work, there had to be a compromise. All of the states knew they had to band together and sacrifice for this experiment to work. And so this passage of the Declaration of Independence was taken out. For if it was not dismissed from this document, there might not have been a country or worse yet a civil war would have happened. What was it like for slavery in the colonies before the generations of people and before the Founders like George Washington were born?

Paul Johnson, a historian from London, says: "Eighteenth-century Virginia in which Washington lived and farmed, was a world in which degrees of servitude were habitual and taken for granted." Johnson also states "Much of the servitude of early America for farming was procured by people working off debts who were sentenced by British courts to terms of a transportation-a minimum of seven years, often fourteen or more- and were hired out to farmers by the State. The third and lowest group were chattel slaves, black or mulatto, mostly sold to Portuguese slave traders by African Kings or chiefs. They were introduced to the British Colonies by the Dutch traders in 1617 and were soon numerous in Virginia, though it was not until South Carolina was colonized from the West Indies that American chattel slavery became an important institution." (Johnson 37,38)

Let's consider the 13th, 14th, and 15th amendments and why they are pivotal to changing the conversation about race. Race and slavery were things that The Founders and Washington didn't know how to change because it was a way of life that came from the British and Dutch around the year 1617 or 1619.

In the many generations before the Founders and George Washington were even born, how could they be found at fault for the institution of slavery, that we ourselves, did not start or institute from the year 1619?

If people were really concerned with slavery in race relations today, they would be talking about how human tracking and slavery still actually happens in other countries, in the world, and not just singling out the United States for its past sins over 240 years ago. But these amendments, the 13th the 14th the 15th, to the Constitution help to procure the end and paradigm shift in freedom for all.

The 13th Amendment states "Neither slavery nor involuntary servitude, except as a punishment for crime whereof the party shall have been duly convicted, shall exist within the United States, or any place subject to their jurisdiction." Now think about the deleted passage from the Declaration of Independence and the 3/5 compromise? This 13th Amendment leaps forward everything that George Washington and the Founders were trying to do. The Founders knew they couldn't put a tight grip on the states and slavery, so they made it available for the future generations to do the right thing. The 13th through 15th amendments solidifies everything that Founders wanted.

How could we blame the Founders for an institution that they didn't start or institute here in the United States? At least the Founders knew it was wrong and planted the seeds to end this way of life. These amendments help to say "no" to an institution that could only be done away with by the seeds planted in the 1700s. It is precisely what the abolitionists of the North who signed the Constitution would have wanted in the first place, to abolish slavery and involuntary servitude. Sometimes good things take time to blossom, and we see a culmination of this in the 14th and 15th amendments. Part of the 14th Amendment was meant for the idea in giving children born of slaves, citizenship who were already here in the states, not illegal immigrants, but natural-born peoples who were born into involuntary servitude, citizenship to the United States.

The concluding Amendment that strengthened the idea of liberty to all peoples in representation part of Article 1 Section 2 of the Constitution is the 15th Amendment. It gives all free persons the right to have a voice and to vote, (this will be concluded with the 19th Amendment). Sometimes these three amendments came at a cost to our infant nation, but they were worth the sacrifice that George Washington made in pledging his whole adult life to give all peoples the opportunity to life liberty and the pursuit of happiness.

For more context, what has the modern age in the 20th century done to hold back the tide of the race relations in the 1960's? What would George Washington have done? In 1961, when President John F. Kennedy signed Executive Order 10925, is most likely what George would have done to bring people together yet again on the issue of race. How many times does a president have to act before the peoples of a nation get their act together? Our past and current presidents all have good and bad things about them. No one is perfect. But these people of stature and power have no bearing on my self-worth or your self-worth or self-esteem as a person. We as a society shouldn't let others determine our self-worth through legislation, especially from a bureaucrat who knows nothing about me or you and our generations of families to come afterward. But this Executive order from JFK funded projects and "takes affirmative action to ensure that applicants are employed, and employees are treated during employment, without regard to their race, creed, color, or national origin." This is bringing people together in some kind of way. I wonder if communities, the entertainment industry, and government officials were taught civility and chivalry if this issue of race would even be a problem today?

The Civil Rights Acts of 1964, 1965, and 1968 did more to procure the fundamental issue plaguing our nation. In 1964 the Civil Rights Act which ended segregation coupled with Civil Rights Act 1965 solidified, even more, the 3/5 compromise and the right to vote for Black Americans. This Civil Rights Act of 1965 signed by President Lyndon B. Johnson, helped overcome legal barriers at the state and local levels that still prevented African Americans from exercising their right to vote as guaranteed under the 15th Amendment to the U.S. Constitution. Our leaders of this country need to reminded of this country's freedom and responsibility to its people. Which, in part, is a responsibility to safeguard our representation of a free nation of people. Concluding with the Civil Rights Act of 1968, which procure the right to all peoples. Doesn't this conversation about race and slavery seem complete after all these laws and founding documents and museums?

What else is there to talk about? There is a museum in Washington D.C. which by the way, is fantastic. If you ever have the chance to see the National Museum of African American History and Culture, I would definitely go check it out. But of course, black lives matter. Of course all lives matter. Why can't groups like the KKK, BLM, ACLU, SEIU movements move forward on this issue of race? It's because they are stuck in the past and fail to recognize the strides of success of this Republic. I guess if people are so unthankful about living in the United States, maybe they should try living somewhere else with their attitude?

Like I said, imagine if the Founders tried to tackle every issue imaginable? Our Constitution would be many volumes long. We most likely wouldn't have had a country to call home had they done that. The Founders were wise in setting up a country based on freedom and the ability for the Constitution to be able to be changed. No matter how long it takes to achieve it and then figure everything else out later. Yes, George Washington and the Founders at times could have done more. A Civil War at the founding of this country surely would have ended this country before it began. The Founders changed their hearts and minds overtime to establish this Republic, not a democracy.

Lincoln helped to solidify the Republic in his image of what he thought was good. People in America have all the opportunities available to change their own destiny and not be chained down to other peoples thoughts if they choose to. Stop letting thoughts that hold you back and put in your mind thoughts of advancement, joy, and success! Anything is possible if you believe. When any group of people, it doesn't matter who they are, can't accept the failures of the past and rejoice in the accomplishments of past generations, we begin to fail. We then fall into the mindset of not having free will to choose your own destiny. We fall into the mindset of not learning from our mistakes and becoming a better people for God and for our country! All the growth that has come since the founding of the country will be undermined if we don't forgive the past. We become people of the world if we don't forgive. I mean if you want the world to like you, then be like the world. Because they, the people who run the world promote division, segregation, and stagnation in human development.

Without the efforts of the Founders to include Washington, who planted the seeds of liberty in the founding documents, we would be stuck permanently in the past. These kinds of people who continually live in the doldrums of the past become feeble and helpless.

All kinds of people still complain without realizing they have it all. What more do people want on the issue of race? Do they want the complete extermination of whites? If people really want to be upset, they should be complaining to the Dutch and British who brought slavery over here to the United States. The only thing left for all parties involved, (that's you and me) that no one has really talked about and really put into action is to raise our children to think rightly, godly, and honorably about others. Yes, sometimes, we will make mistakes. That's life. Some people don't want to take responsibility for teaching their children to think the best in people. Therefore there will always be a problem between races if we don't teach the younger generation to think the best. The children of this country are our future. What kind of future do we want our kids to live in? To move forward when someone doesn't want to comprise, especially when discussing politics is not being rude. The Founders and George did. How do you think this Republic was founded? On compromise! Why can't you compromise? If George Washington were alive today, he would be disgusted with the continuous division about race and how far we've come and are still arguing. In his farewell address, George said:

"The name of American, which belongs to you, in your national capacity, must always exalt the just pride of patriotism, more than any appellation derived from local discriminations."

We are all Americans, and we all must move forward sooner rather than later to procure the country that George gave everything for. Some people would instead take the easy way out and succumb to current political bias and stereotypes and propionate the problem of race.

The only way to leap out of this issue is to attack it from the source. From the mind and heart. Habits matter. And we have to as a society teach our children to do the right thing, try your best, and live honorably, godly and chivalrously towards others just as Augustus and Mary Ball Washington did for George. That's the only way to overcome this issue. George Washington understood that great things take time. He was a patient man. But he demanded respect and loyalty when given the responsibility for fathering this nation.

BIBLIOGRAPHY

Allen, Thomas B., and Cheryl Harness. George Washington, Spymaster: How America Outspied the British and Won the Revolutionary War. National Geographic, 2004.

Avlon, John P. Washington's Farewell: The Founding Father's Warning to Future Generations. Simon & Schuster, 2017.

Beck, Glenn, and Kevin Balfe. Being George Washington: The Indispensable Man, as You've Never Seen Him. Threshold Editions/Mercury Radio Arts, 2012.

Brady, Patricia. Martha Washington: an American Life. Penguin Books, 2006.

Breen, T. H. George Washington's Journey: The President Forges a New Nation. Simon & Schuster, 2017.

Chernow, Ron. Washington: a Life. Penguin Books, 2011.

Connell, Janice T. The Spiritual Journey of George Washington. CreateSpace, 2013.

Dershowitz, Alan. *The Case For Israel* John Wiley &sons, Inc 2003

Ellis, Joseph J. His Excellency: George Washington. Alfred A. Knopf, 2011.

George Washington's Mount Vernon: Official Guidebook. Mount Vernon Ladies' Association, 2017.

Henriques, Peter R. Realistic Visionary: a Portrait of George Washington. University of Virginia Press, 2006.

Johnson, Paul. George Washington: the Founding Father. Harper Perennial, 2005.

Kapp, Friedrich The Life of Frederick William Von Steuben, Major General In the Revolutionary Army, 1859

Ketchum, Richard M. The World of George Washington. American Heritage Publishing, 1974.

Kilmeade, Brian, and Don Yaeger. George Washington's Secret Six: the Spy Ring That Saved the American Revolution. Sentinel, 2013.

Lengel, Edward G. First Entrepreneur: How George Washington Built His--and the Nation's--Prosperity. Da Capo Press, a Member of the Perseus Books Group, 2016.

Lengel, Edward G. Inventing George Washington: America's Founder, in Myth and Memory. Harper, 2011.

Lengel, Edward G. General George Washington: A Military Life. Random House Trade Paperbacks, 2007.

Lockhart, Paul Douglas. The Drillmaster of Valley Forge: the Baron De Steuben and the Making of the American Army. Harper, 2010.

Novak, Michael, and Jana Novak. Washington's God: Religion, Liberty, and the Father of Our Country. A Member of the Perseus Books Group, 2006.

Pelton, Robert W. George Washington's Prayers. Freedom & Liberty Foundation Press, 2017.

Randall, Willard Sterne. George Washington: A Life. Henry Holt and Company LLC, 1997.

Rhodehamel, John. George Washington: The Wonder of the Age. Yale University Press, 2017.

Rice, Condoleezza. *No Higher Honor: a Memoir of My Years in Washington*. Crown Publishers, 2011.

Rice, Condoleezza. *Democracy: Stories from the Long Road to Freedom.* Twelve, 2017.

Stark, Peter. Young Washington: How Wilderness and War Forged America's Founding Father. Ecco, 2018.

Unger, Harlow G."Mr. President": George Washington and the Making of the Nation's Highest Office. Da Capo Press, 2013.

Washington, Austin. The Education of George Washington How a Forgotten Book Shaped the Character of a Hero. Regnery Publishing, 2014.

Washington, George, and W. B. Allen. George Washington: A Collection. Liberty Fund Inc., 1988.

Washington, George, and Paul M. Zall. Washington on Washington. University Press of Kentucky, 2003.

Washington, George. Quotations of George Washington. Applewood Books, 2003.

Wiencek, Henry. An Imperfect God George Washington, His Slaves, and the Creation of America. Farrar, Straus and Giroux, 2003.

REFERENCE NOTES

Real Fake News:
https://www.smithsonianmag.com/history/ag
eold-problem-fake-news-180968945/

https://www.bbc.com/news/blogstrending-
42724320

https://psmag.com/social-justice/how-
trumpweaponized-fake-news-for-his-own-
political-ends

https://www.cnbc.com/2018/10/10/the-
fakenews-tag-has-given-street-cred-to-mass-
disbelief-bbc-director-general-says.html

Steuben's time in America:
https://www.americanheritage.com/content/d
rillmaster-valley-forge

https://www.thenation.com/article/we-
colonialssodomy-laws-america/

1996 court case:
https://legal-dictionary.thefreedictionary.com/
Defense+of+Marriage+Act+of+1996

https://www.govtrack.us/congress/bills/104/hr3396/summary
2015 court case:
https://www.nytimes.com/interactive/2015/us/2014-term-supreme-court-decision-same-sexmarriage.html

https://en.wikipedia.org/wiki/Obergefell_v._Hodges#cite_note-108

How bills become laws:
 https://www.usa.gov/how-laws-are-made
Federalist papers

https://www.history.com/topics/early-us/federalist-papers

https://www.loc.gov/rr/program/bib/ourdocs/ federalist.html

https://www.constitutionfacts.com/us-articles-ofconfederation/the-federalist-papers/

Complete Charlottesville Transcript:
https://www.latimes.com/politics/la-na-pol-trump-charlottesville-transcript-20170815-story.html

https://thehill.com/opinion/white-house/456523-donald-trumps-no-racist-as-past-acts-and-presidential-record-prove

Trump's "very fine people" on both sides:
https://www.realclearpolitics.com/articles/201
9/03/21/trump_didnt_call_neo-
nazis_fine_people_heres_proof_139815.html

https://abcnews.go.com/Politics/trump-lashes-
alt-left-charlottesville-fine-people-
sides/story?id=49235032

https://www.theatlantic.com/politics/archive/
2017/08/trump-defends-white-nationalist-
protesters-some-very-fine-people-on-both-
sides/537012/

Trump blames both sides:
https://www.nationalreview.com/2017/08/tru
mp-blame-both-sides-charlottesville-statement-
factual-correct-description-trump/

https://www.realclearpolitics.com/articles/201
9/08/06/america_is_drowning_in_the_lefts_lies
_about_trump_140950.html

Holding back the Tide sources Jefferson's note:
https://founders.archives.gov/documents/
Jefferson/01-28-02-0441

The 3/5 compromise:
https://www.britannica.com/topic/The-FoundingFathers-and-Slavery-1269536

https://www.bethepeopletv.com/attacking-ourfounders/

https://emorywheel.com/the-three-fthscompromise-in-context/

https://www.bethepeopletv.com/attacking-ournations-founders/

https://constitutioncenter.org/interactiveconstitution/amendments/amendment-xiii

Deleted Passage of DOI sources:
https://blackpast.org/primary/declarationindependence-and-debate-over-slavery

https://www.washington.edu/news/2016/02/25/documents-that-changed-the-world-thedeclaration-of-independences-deleted-passage-on slavery-1776/

Thomas Jefferson, The Writings of Thomas Jefferson: Being His Autobiography, Correspondence, Reports, Messages, Addresses, and other Writings, Official and Private (Washington, D.C.: Taylor & Maury, 1853-1854).

Religious Tolerance Sources:
https://founders.archives.gov/documents/Washington/05-05-02-0193

https://founders.archives.gov/documents/Washington/05-06-02-0135

https://www.archives.gov/legislative/features/gwinauguration

Worry about yourself sources:
https://www.wsj.com/articles/SB10000872396390443404004577578910457017318

https://www.jpost.com/Features/In-Thespotlight/ This-Week-In-History-The-Arab-Leagues-three-nos

https://factly.in/united-nations-budgetcontributions-by-member-countries/

www.ingramcontent.com/pod-product-compliance
Lightning Source LLC
Chambersburg PA
CBHW060422290526
45791CB00002B/849